WONDERS!
Our World in Fact and Fiction

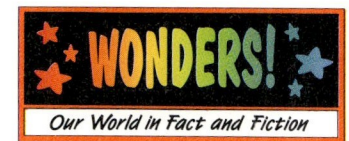

# Homes Are for Living

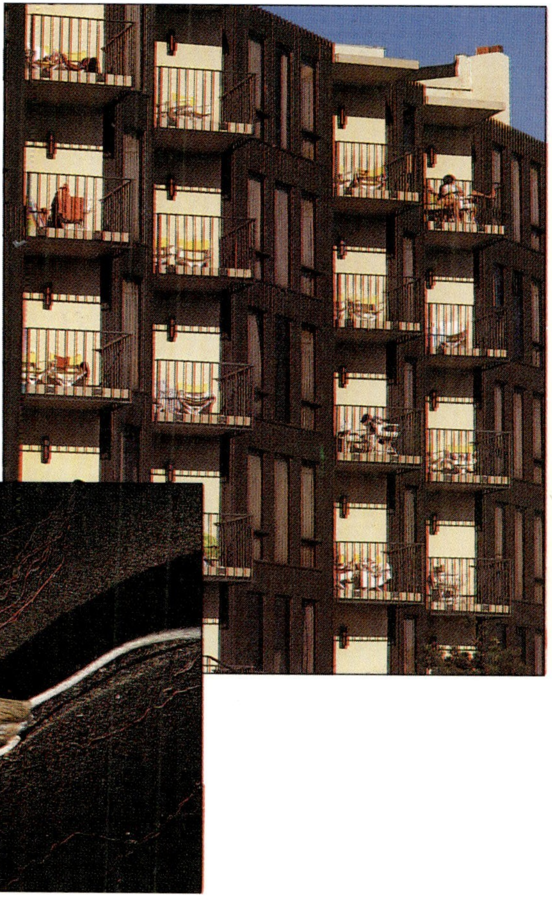

Ina Cumpiano

illustrated with photographs

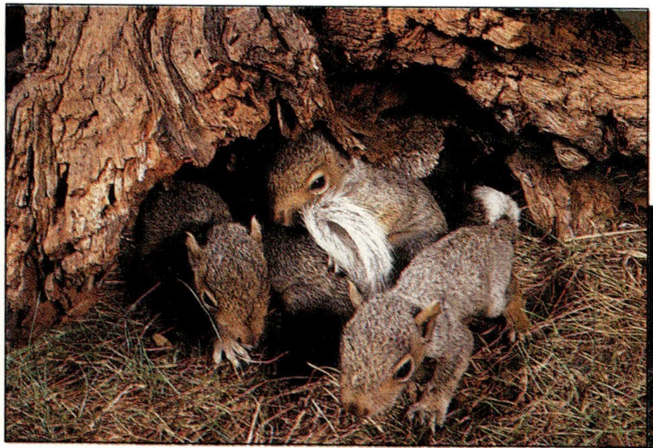

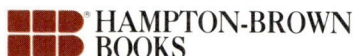

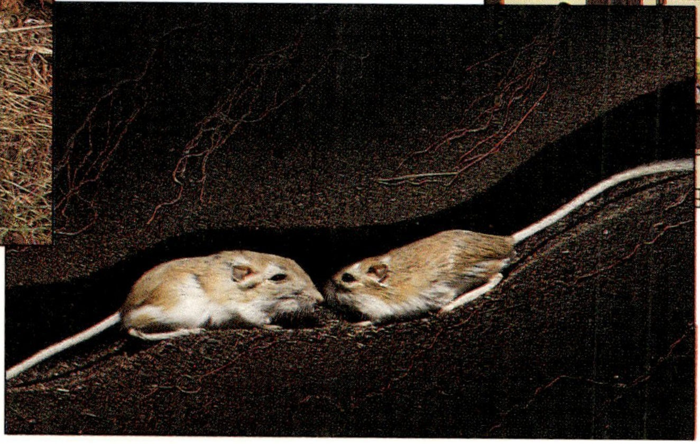

HAMPTON-BROWN BOOKS

Copyright © 1991 Hampton-Brown Books
All rights reserved. No part of this book may be reproduced or transmitted in any form or by any means, electronic or mechanical, including photocopying, recording or by an information storage and retrieval system, without permission in writing from the Publisher.

Hampton-Brown Books
P.O. Box 223220
Carmel, California 93922

Printed in the United States of America
ISBN 1–56334–053–4

96 97 98 99 00 10 9 8 7 6 5 4 3 2

**Illustrations:** Sharron O'Neil
**Photographs:** AllStock: cover (igloo), p. 22a; Animals/Animals: cover inset (fish), back cover insets (raccoons, beaver), pp. 1a, 2a, 3a, 3c, 6, 7b, 12a, 12b, 12c, 13, 14; Earth Scenes: back cover insets (Manhattan, Kenya), pp. 2b, 3b, 9b, 15, 23b, 23c, 24a, 24b, 24c; Photo Researchers: cover insets (owl, sampans), back cover inset (kangaroo rats), pp. 1b, 1c, 7a, 8a, 8b, 9a, 18, 19a, 19b, 20, 22b, 23a

Animals and humans live in many different kinds of homes. Homes differ depending on who lives in them and where they are.

# WHO LIVES IN THE CITY?

The city is a place full of people and activity. There are tall buildings where many people live. Animals live in the city, too. Some are pets that live in their owners' homes. Others are wild animals that live outdoors.

squirrel

nest in a hole in a tree

pigeon

hummingbird

mockingbird

butterfly

nest of twigs

## THAT'S A FACT!

Swallows eat and drink while they are flying. To eat, they open their huge mouths and catch insects in midair. When they want to drink, they swoop down to a puddle or a stream and, without landing, dip their beaks in the water.

One wild animal that lives in cities is the swallow. Swallows often make nests under the eaves of buildings. They build them by sticking together hundreds of little mud balls. Each nest is bottle-shaped, with the entrance facing downward.

Squirrels also live in cities. They live in parks and neighborhoods where there are trees. Like swallows, squirrels make nests. They make them in the trunks of trees or high in the branches.

These baby squirrels have just come out of their nest.

## Hands On

Talk with your classmates about the pets that each of you has at home. Make a chart like this one to show how many of each kind of animal the class has.

| PETS IN THE HOME | | | | |
|---|---|---|---|---|
| cats | Mary | Mary | John | |
| dogs | Mary | John | Paco | Eve |
| fish | Eve | Paco | | |
| birds | Paco | | | |

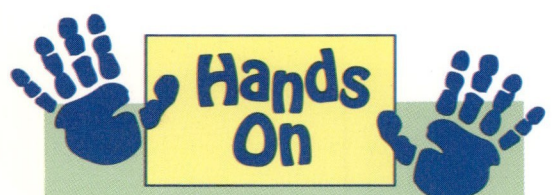

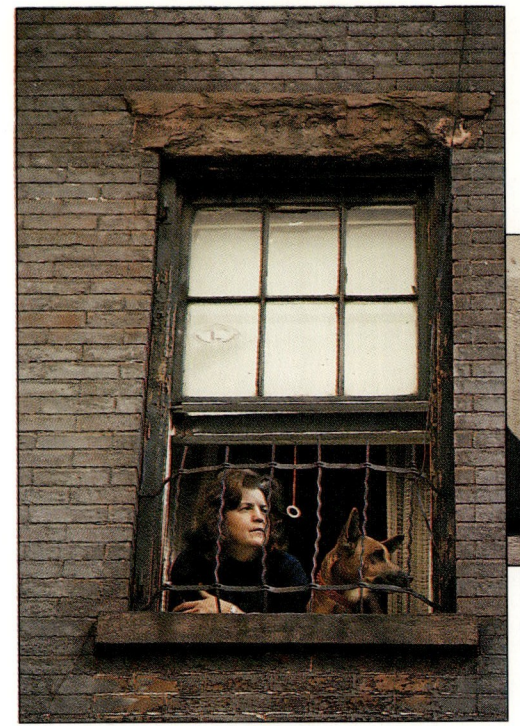

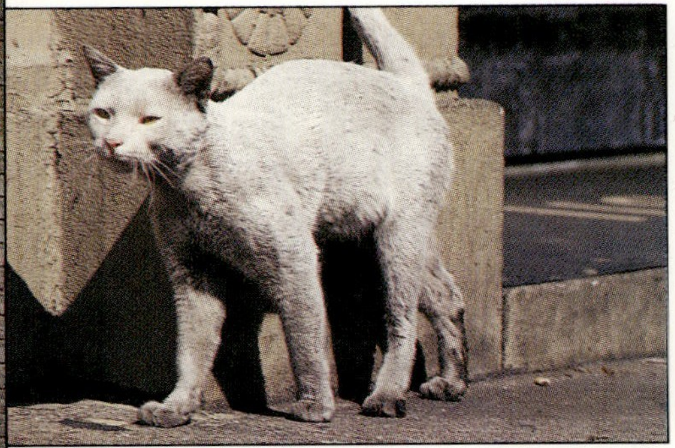

Most of the cats and dogs that live in the city are pets. They live in houses or apartments with their owners, who take care of them and feed them.

If you also live in a city, maybe you live in an **apartment house** like this one. In apartment houses, many people can live in a small area. That is important in a city because space is very valuable.

The president of the United States lives in the city of Washington, D.C. His house is called the White House.

## WHO LIVES IN THE FOREST?

The forest is dark and cool because the trees block out much of the sunlight. Many animals live in the forest. Some live in the trees. Others live in caves and rivers.

10

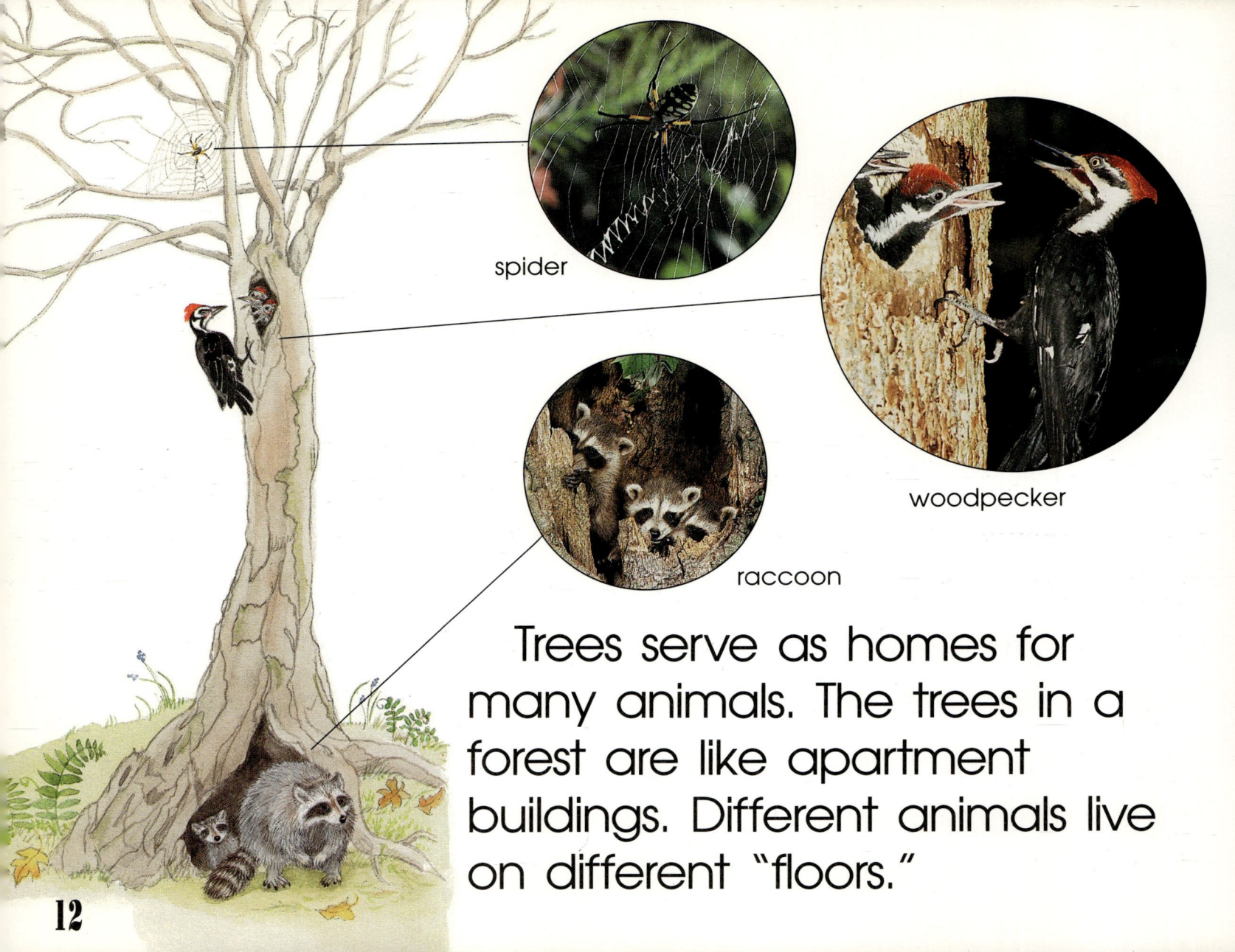

spider

woodpecker

raccoon

Trees serve as homes for many animals. The trees in a forest are like apartment buildings. Different animals live on different "floors."

12

The black bear also lives in the forest. In the fall, it makes a **den**, or home, in a cave or under the roots of a tree. In its den, it makes a bed of twigs and leaves. That's where it sleeps through the winter.

Beavers live in streams. They build a dam with sticks and branches. They build their lodges in the pond the dam creates.

The entrance to a lodge is underwater. The beaver family lives in a dry and cozy room above the water level.

People also live in the forest. Sometimes they make their homes out of logs because it is easy to get logs in the forest. Do you think you would like to live in a log cabin?

### Hands On

Here's how to make a log cabin with a partner:

- Cut a door and a window in a small box.
- Glue twigs onto the sides of the box.
- Make a roof out of a piece of cardboard folded in half and glue the roof on the cabin.

# WHO LIVES IN THE DESERT?

It is very hot in the desert during the day. That is why many desert animals come out only at night, when it is cooler. In the daytime, they hide in their caves, burrows, or nests in order to escape the hot sun.

woodpecker

elf owl

nest

iguana

In the desert there are owls that live in holes in cactuses. These holes are made by woodpeckers. These owls come out only at night, when they search for insects to eat.

This little animal also lives in the desert. It's a kangaroo rat. How do you think it got its name?

Kangaroo rats make little sand hills full of holes. The holes are entrances to their home, which is underground.

Kangaroo rats in a tunnel in their underground home

**COYOTE DEN**

A coyote's den is a "room" at the end of a very long tunnel. This is where the mother coyote has her pups. Coyotes are famous for their nighttime howling.

Ahoo-oo-oo!

Some people who live in the desert have homes with thick **adobe** walls. Adobe walls keep the house cool when it's hot and cozy when it's cold.

## Hands On

Adobe is mud mixed with straw which is used to make bricks. The bricks are shaped in wooden molds and then set out in the sun to dry. Adobe bricks can also be baked in a kiln.

You can make your own "adobe" shapes. Moisten some dirt until it has the consistency of modeling clay. Then mix in bits of dry grass. Make shapes with the "adobe," using cookie molds, and put them out in the sun to dry.

21

# All Around the World

Houses vary according to the part of the world where they are found. The kind of house built in a particular place depends on the climate and the materials available there.

Hong Kong is a city where many, many people live. Some of them live on **houseboats** in the port.

In northern Alaska, where it snows a lot and there are no trees, people make **igloos** out of large blocks of ice or snow.

23

Mud is abundant in this African village. Houses are built from mud and other materials.

In this village on a river in Indonesia, houses are built on **stilts** to keep them above the water.

In the deserts of Iran, there are people who live in **tents** made of black felt. The tents can be easily put up and taken down. This is important, since these people frequently move from one place to another.

## WHERE DO YOU LIVE?

In a city?
In a small town?
In a cold place, or in a hot place?
How is your house suited to the place where you live?

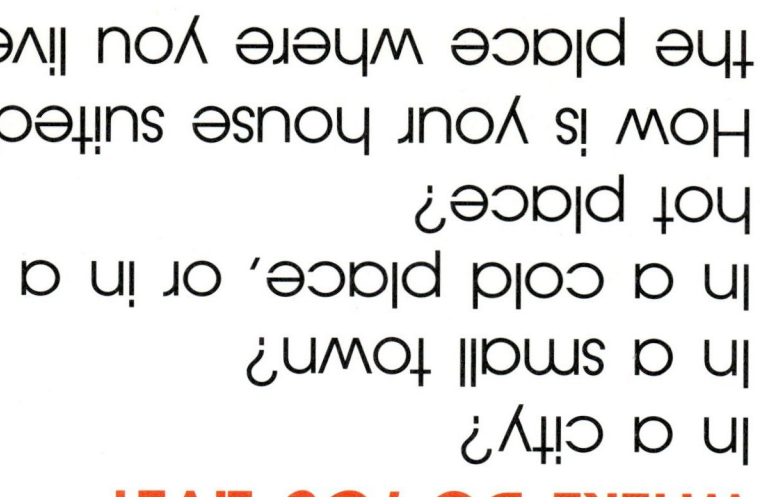